Departure of the Sea

Departure of the Sea

Stories about Kuwait in the Eyes of a Kuwaiti Woman

Haifa Al Sanousi, Ph.D.

Translated by
Anchi Hoh, Ph.D.

To order additional copies of this book, contact:
Xlibris Corporation
1-888-795-4274
www.Xlibris.com
Orders@Xlibris.com
52585

Contents

Dedication

To a Kuwaiti lady who came from the old Kuwait, carrying with her
ocean breeze, ancestral root, and filled with integrity and purity.
She was a moral dictionary that was difficult to find.
She greeted us farewell and left us as quietly as she came to this world.
She left for an unknown world.
I dedicate this book to her, along with my thoughts
for her and for the breezes that she carried.

Acknowledgments

I would like to thank Haifa Al Sanousi for offering me this opportunity to translate this collection of eight short stories. The research effort I spent in writing my doctoral thesis for the University of Manchester, U.K, entitled "Contemporary Short Stories by Women Writers in Kuwait, from the 1970s to the Present," has helped me establish a decent understanding of the struggles and challenges women in Kuwait faced through women's literature. Al Sanousi's stories transcend beyond women's issues and demonstrate a broader concern for humanity.

My thanks also go to Karam Habashy, a respected colleague who has helped me with my Arabic. It should also be noted that Matthew Hogan did a fantastic job in editing my translation. Finally, I would like to thank my family for their constant support and encouragement.

Introduction

Haifa Al Sanousi, Her Stories and Kuwait: Reclaiming Islam and Redefining Feminism

Anchi Hoh, Ph.D.

Since the advent of the Qissah Qasirah (short story) genre in Kuwait, along with the establishment of newspapers and journals in the 1930s, the number of women writing short stories in Kuwait has been steadily increasing. The 1970s saw the rise of Layla al-'Uthman (b. 1945), one of the best-known Kuwaiti female writers in the West; others include Fatimah Yusuf al-Ali (b. 1953), Thuraya al-Baqsami (b. 1952), Wafa' al-Hamdan (b. 19??), Tibah al-Ibrahim (b. 1944?), Layla Muhammad Salih (b. 19??), Haifa Al Sanousi (b. 1963), Muna al-Shafei (b. 1946), and Aliya Shuayb (b. 1964).[1]

Having continued to apply the original function of social criticism of this literary genre, Kuwaiti women writers quickly realized their yearning for self-awareness and self-analysis, which coincided with the feminist movement in the West, may very well be substantiated in their story writing. Thus, the subjects they write about range from women's self-reflection through representations of family, love, and sexuality, and continue on to social criticism, and the dramatic sweep of war and nationalism. These stories not only offer in-depth examinations of the lives of women and their relationships with family and society, but also

---

[1] For a comprehensive analysis of Kuwaiti women writers known in the short story genre, see Anchi Hoh, "Contemporary Short Stories by Women Writers in Kuwait," PhD dissertation, University of Manchester, 2005.

provide fertile ground for those interested in women's studies to witness and examine the significant development of Kuwaiti women's self-identity. Each of the aforementioned writers focuses on a specific range of topics, becoming unique in their own way. Holistically, each author's individual style, belief, and approach join to create the mosaic which constitutes the portrait of women's literature in Kuwait; it would be a grave mistake to think that the women writers in this small country are of one mind.

Many writers appear to have influences derived from the West, others from the former Soviet Union. In the midst of her contemporaries, Haifa Al Sanousi's writing is likely to give readers a glimpse of the complexity of Kuwaiti women's literature and lives. Her writings represent a voice different from those influenced by Western or by Soviet-Marxist discourse for she seeks to define Arab women's identity independent of ideological or prevailing feminist norms.

About the Author and Her Writings

Known for a long time as a critic, researcher, Kuwait University lecturer, and therapeutic writing workshop leader, Al Sanousi added one more identity in 2000, that of literary writer when she published her first collection of short stories, *Women in A Swirl*.[2] Her continuous endeavors later won the recognition and encouragement of Prof. Mustafa Mahmoud, a famous Egyptian scholar and writer in his eighties. The collection, written deliberately in English in order to communicate with Western readers, delineated diverse dilemmas and struggles facing Kuwaiti women in everyday life, including the notable tension that strains their relationships with men in their family and in society at large. On a more cursory examination, the collection might be taken to be an echo of some of Layla al-'Uthman's writings, with their characteristic highlighting of Arab women's victimization in a patriarchal society. But contrary to that initial impression, Al Sanousi intended to show that the Arab women's struggle is no more unique than that of any other. As a result, she questioned the need to exaggerate Arab women's problems. To better advance that perspective, Al Sanousi chose to write the entire collection in English—a rare effort among Kuwaiti women writers and indeed, in general Kuwaiti literary circles.

Al Sanousi is also one of the few who highlight the Islamic influence on Muslims' lives in literature. Prayers and religious expressions often appear in her stories in various conditions in life and their effects on the characters' psychological statuses. Consequently, readers get a realistic sense of Muslim life from the author's female perspective and note how culture and religion

---

[2] *Women in A Swirl: A Collection of Short Stories*, [Kuwait]: n.p., 2000.

are intertwined in Kuwaiti society. To the author, the incorporation of religious elements into her writing comes naturally because religion is part of her life and the society she lives in, and therefore has unavoidably become one of the foundations of her creativity.

Sexuality is a popular subject among women writers; their heroines often embark on a journey of sexual self-discovery. Sexuality also plays an important part in many Kuwaiti women writers' stories, such as those of Layla al-'Uthman, Fatima Yusuf al-Ali, and Alia Shuaib. Western feminist literary critics believe that writing about female sexuality as a means of self-examination leads to the confirmation of female identity. That idea has two implications: first, that female sexuality is essentially different from male sexuality, and second, that female sexuality (as feminists claim) has been completely ignored or misinterpreted in the context of patriarchal culture worldwide. By recognizing female sexuality, feminist theory asserts that the prevailing values and attitudes toward women in the current patriarchal cultures and systems are challenged and even threatened. It is intriguing that Al Sanousi has never felt the need to deal with sexuality in her writing. Although respectful of the Western feminist efforts, she seriously questions those who have always followed these trends and never transcend beyond them. To Al Sanousi and probably her generation, recognizing female sexuality in the search for female self-identity is out-of-date. A woman's identity should be sought beyond that stage and be seen as part of the greater national and cultural identity she belongs to. Failure to do so seems to lead to self-imposed marginalization.

> "I have to say that I am not convinced of the value of writing about female sexuality . . . I have always wondered if female sexuality is a [valid] means for examining and recognizing women's own physical and emotional feelings and senses. I think the answer is no. There are many political, social, and psychological issues that can be found in the writings of both women and men. Women should pass through the barriers and not limit their writings to sexual identity. Most of the women writers who are writing about these issues are repeating themselves; they never stop focusing on sexuality. I wonder why they surround themselves in sexual imagery. Is it just to attract readers and critics to their writing?"[3]

So instead of emphasizing the inward search for female sexuality as part of the female identity, Al Sanousi demonstrates in her stories that an Arab Muslim woman's self-confidence and self-realization are intertwined with

---

[3] Haifa Al Sanousi, personal interview by mail, February 2006.

religious faith, national identity, and humanity. She directs readers' attention to the humanistic part of her writing. "I am reflecting my thoughts and feeling as a human being," she observes, "and not only as a woman."[4]

Al Sanousi's condemnation of human cruelty and yearning for social justice, peace, and humanity are underscored in the poem, "Mess, Mess, Mess!!!"[5]

> The Satan slumbers . . .
>
> But still . . .
> The demons of mankind arise
> To burn the world
> To show their powers.
>
> Oh—the man!
> —The black hearted evil
> Rousing all bad wizards, bad witches
> Residing in between the red walls
> Imprisoning the one big lament
> To cast their devil spell
>
> The horror party begins
> Evil's dancing on dead corpses
> Tasting the fleeing blood
> And there is no love just the mud . . .
>
> But still . . .
> Somewhere, there is the mountain
> Blossoming in green
> Good people there and here.
> Peace and justice in their eyes
> And love—love that's the one
> That never dies.

For those who are interested in the evolution of Arab women's writings and the feminist thoughts reflected in Arab women's literature, Al Sanousi's attempt to incorporate the Islamic faith in her writings and interest in emphasizing humanity from a woman's perspective are noteworthy because she presents

---

[4] Ibid.

[5] Haifa Al Sanousi, personal interview by mail, February 15, 2006.

a perspective different from the ones offered by other Arab women writers preceded her.

As a short story writer who has experienced firsthand the interaction between Islam and the West, religion and feminism, tradition and Westernization, Al Sanousi is certainly well-qualified to take on a broader mission: to show Western readers a little-known side of Kuwait (and of Muslims in general), and the concerns that affect that society. Moreover, throughout her stories, an intriguing and compelling literary image of Kuwait takes shape.

About *Departure of the Sea*

Inspired by, and dedicated to Al Sanousi's deceased mother, this collection is often engaged in reminiscing the period in which her mother lived. It puts forth a set of virtues from those times, delineating values and ethics that the author laments no longer exist. The stories are imbued with the humanity of the people of Kuwait and the Arab world, as well as their sociopolitical concerns.

Departure of the Sea collects eight short stories, each focusing on a different social phenomenon or relationship. The issues addressed can be divided roughly into two sub-areas: family and society. On the subject of family, several types of relationships are highlighted, including father-daughter, husband-wife, and mother-daughter. These categories often appear negative in many other stories, but not in Al Sanousi's. As to the exploration of Kuwaiti society, Al Sanousi addresses various themes that provide an in-depth look into her oil-rich country. Her prose takes on religion, attachment to the past and to the sea, social dysfunction, as well as racial tensions in Kuwait that the Western audience may find interesting.

The title story, "Rahil al-Bahr" ("Departure of the Sea"), describes the many virtues of earlier times as seen through an old woman's recollection of her life. On her deathbed, Fidhah recalls a series of bittersweet episodes from her youth. Her old house was not fancy but provided a shelter of love and warmth. The sister of a young girl who always escaped housework to play with other children and of another child who was too mentally disabled to take care of herself, Fidhah develops early on a strong sense of responsibility. As much as she wanted to play with other children, she never refused her mother's orders to do housework as she empathized with her plight.

> "My poor mother was always troubled by Aishah's retardation and Nurah's extreme misbehavior.
>
> I was wise despite my youth. I did want to play with Nurah and her friends, but I pitied my mother who was continuously fulfilling her

endless responsibilities. I felt it was necessary to help her with the
burdens of the house.

—Darn that Nurah! She went off to play just like that. Fidhah, you
are a sweetheart. Was I too harsh on you when I left you to bake
bread? . . .

I interrupted her:

—No, no. I am happy to do this. I hope you stop repeating
expressions like this. I feel very happy helping you. I also like to
do the housework.

—But Nurah . . .

I interrupted her again:

—Nurah is still young. Let her play.

I hid my feelings and tried not to show my own strong desire to play
with Nurah and her friends.

The punishment for Nurah's disobedience was a fall off a swing, which
injured her nose and only barely eluded discovery and rebuke by her father; the
reward for being an obedient child was that Fidhah received repeated praise
and honor, and was blessed by God with a nice family in her adult life. At the
end of the story, the elderly Fidhah dies surrounded by loving children and
grandchildren. Like the sea that surrounded Kuwait and provided its lifelines,
Fidhah symbolizes the noble people and ethics of the past. She is clearly also
the literary incarnation of Al Sanousi's mother.

Certain traditional items of clothing or work are mentioned and help
readers form a better picture of the way people looked and behaved. These
objects, including the bakhnaq (a kind of headscarf worn by young girls), milfa'
(a kind of headscarf women wore in the past), and diram (a kind of lipstick
used by women in the past), were integral parts of Kuwaiti history that today
are most probably relegated only to museums or history books.

Death appears in another story, "Irtihal" ("Departure"). A young boy takes
center stage in this melancholic tale. Poor health has led to the child's low
self-esteem and consequently prevents the boy from making friends with other
children. He becomes acquainted with the sea, which by nature is unprejudiced
and discriminates against no one. Unfortunately, the sea also symbolizes
the hoped-for future that the boy will ultimately never know. Nevertheless,

Al Sanousi's young character sees the sea as "the bridge to his dreams and ambitions" and decides to entrust all of these dreams and ambitions to a paper boat. He gives this boat the chance to risk the journey to that unknown future, a chance he would never have. To the boy and the author, the sea was "the unlimited world of dreams."[6]

This collection of short stories also calls attention to a number of controversial social issues, about which Al Sanousi offers her perceptions, setting herself uniquely apart from other women writers. These include gender relations, the sensitive interaction between Kuwaitis and other Arabs, racial discrimination and its impact, and the challenge of terrorism and the reactions to it.

In the following two stories, "Shay' min al-Wahm" ("Delusions") and "Hurub" ("Escape"), readers will notice that Al Sanousi does not present women as victims in relationships as many women writers are inclined to do. The stories suggest two very interesting and practical observations: First, men and women both are responsible for the wellness of their relationships and seeking solutions for solving problems. Neither one is a sole victim who could therefore blame the other for all the unhappiness; Second, women are as capable as men of victimizing their partners.

In "Shay' min al-Wahm" ("Delusions"), a husband and wife do not stand on equal footing, which leads to the crumbling of their marriage. The major cause is the husband's belief that he was smarter and superior having obtained higher education while his wife had only a high school diploma. His arrogance blinds him to the value of what he already does possess; he chooses instead to focus on his life's negative side. Constant insults and abusive comments create a living hell for his wife whose only safe escape is to create her own virtual reality from watching romance films and soap operas. In that virtual reality, the female enjoys the love and respect she lacks in the real world. Her delusions become a place of safety after each episode of her husband's verbal abuse.

Al Sanousi describes her heroine as "a symbol of the woman who was full of dreams but couldn't reach any of them." The result of both members of the couple being ruled by their delusions and negative thoughts was the breakdown of their marriage. A final separation is hinted at the end of the story.

The impact of soap operas in this story should not go unnoticed. Interestingly, the influence of soap operas has become a research topic for several Arab women scholars. Lila Abu-Lughod has looked at the Egyptian soap operas to examine the roles of female producers, actresses, as well as their impact on female audience. Scrutinizing the interaction between these programs and women from various social strata, economic levels, and the

---

6   Haifa Al Sanousi, personal interview by mail, February 24, 2006.

programs' values, she has found that they are very influential despite their emphasis on middle class ideologies and traditional morality. The interaction between media and the female audience is dynamic and complex, Abu-Lughod notes, and that finds an echo in Al Sanousi's fiction.[7]

In "Hurub" ("Escape"), Al Sanousi describes a man's painful failure in his relationships with women. Initially hurt by a failed first marriage and further victimized by his second wife's adultery, the protagonist tries various means to heal his wounds, including seeking solutions from self-help books, going through physical examinations, and taking other steps towards self-improvement. But after several unsuccessful attempts, he finally gives in to the inner voice that constantly undermines his confidence. He decides to escape to another place, hoping to find relief. Internally, however, his doubts keep him unsure of whether escape is an adequate solution. Through this character, Al Sanousi underscored that human beings suffer from unsuccessful relationships regardless of gender, and that women too can inflict tremendous damage to men in inter-gender relationships.

"Al-Intizar" ("Waiting") describes the favoritism that Kuwaitis have to come to accept in a society where many jobs are carried out by foreign expatriates.[8] An old Kuwaiti man undergoing intense physical pain waits an unduly long time for his doctor's appointment, always being preempted by expatriates from other Arab countries. The nurse, an expatriate Arab, abuses her power as the doctor's gatekeeper by showing favoritism to other expatriates. She is also rude to several Asian patients, even as she gives a big smile to a man of her own nationality. Undoubtedly, there have been many studies and much literature written about the victimization and mistreatment of foreign expatriates by the powerful and advantage takers in the Gulf countries and Kuwait as a whole has not been able to earn much sympathy in this matter. However, what has not been asked is: how do ordinary Kuwaitis feel about living in a society like this? Al Sanousi's story is seen as an attempt to offer an answer to that question. As ordinary as her character, the best action he could take is to complain about the tensions between the various ethnic groups present in Kuwait and to naively reminisce the old times prior to the discovery of the oil.

---

[7]   Lila Abu-Lughod, "On- and Off-Camera in Egyptian Soap Operas: Women, Television, and the Public Sphere," *On Shifting Ground: Muslim Women in the Global Era*, ed. Fereshteh Nouraie-Simone, New York: The Feminist Press at the City University of New York, 2005, pp. 16-35.

[8]   According to the *Annual Statistics Year 2001*, compiled by the Ministry of Planning Statistics & Information Sector, the Kuwaitis were 38% of its population of 2.2 million, as opposed to 63% of foreign expatriates (*http://www.mop.gov. kw/mopwebsite/statpdf2001/main%20page.pdf*, accessed January 2, 2007).

In "Man Yasma' Sauti" ("Who Listens to My Voice?"), Al Sanousi's heroine comes from a foreign family of a low social class. Her mother was a housekeeper for many families; her father worked very hard, experienced much hardship and eventually died. The heroine was constantly conscious of her dark skin and different appearance because of hostile looks. She was the recipient of so many discriminatory and suspicious remarks that self-hatred took hold, a state of mind represented by the appearance of bothersome bugs and insects.

> "I closed my eyes. Something quickly passed by—a little bug flying in front of me. I stayed away. How disgusting bugs were! I opened my eyes.
>
> —Umm Khalid, may God repay her. She gave me these nice clothes for you. They were her daughter Hissah's.
>
> My mother showed me the clothes. Her image faded and voice vanished. I dived headlong into another world.
>
> We lived in garbage. Lots of garbage. Disgusting insects always flew in front of me. I couldn't get rid of them or kill them all off. I would kill some everyday.
>
> Had we become part of this country? No. Those harassing looks made sure that we were not one of them.
>
> I had forgotten my dialect and old identity. Or perhaps I was trying to forget everything.
>
> Those annoying insects stayed with me, accompanying me and living inside me."[9]

The story suggests that the heroine was psychologically inflicted by social pressures and by rejection. Only after undergoing psychiatric treatment and being encouraged by a teacher who came from the same country did she slowly gain confidence in herself.

Many women writers have dealt with the issue of foreigners in Kuwait from various vantage points. The foreign group in women's literature ranges from foreign workers to other non-Kuwaiti Arabs. Layla al-'Uthman wrote about Palestinians and their lives and challenges in Kuwait in "Kull al-Aydi Mutashabihah" ("All Hands Are Alike")[10] and in "Yanfasil al-Watan . . .

---

[9] Al Sanusi (2005), pp. 83-5.

[10] Layla al-'Uthman, "Kullal- Aydi Mutashabihah" ("All Hands Are Alike"), *Halat Hubb Majnuna* ("The Status of Love Is Crazy"), n.p.: al-Hay'a al-Misriyah al-'Ammah lil-Jitab, 1989, pp. 91-9.

Tanfasil al-Tariq" ("The Nation Is Divided . . . The Road Is Divided");[11] Muna al-Shafi'i wrote about a foreign maid abused by her Kuwaiti master in "Akhir al-Masa'at" ("The Last Evil Deed");[12] and Wafa' al-Hamdan described the tragic story of a female expatriate and the revenge of her mother in "al-Daf' bil-Umla al-Sa'bah" ("Payment in Hard Currency").[13] What differentiates Al-Sanousi from other women writers is that she chooses to write from a different angle. Namely, she describes her heroine's suffering and subsequent efforts to integrate into society from the perspective of the foreign woman herself instead of telling the story as a distant observer. Through the internalized perspective of the heroine, the reader apprehends the self-hatred, the difficult choice of abandoning an old identity, and the struggle for self-identity as an alien in Kuwaiti society. However, the controversy Al Sanousi raises is that by highlighting the heroine's psychological turmoil, she implicitly doubts the loyalty of resident foreigners to Kuwait and fears the consequent psychological instability as a potential threat to the general safety of the society. Although such observations projected through the story are indeed unfair and controversial accusations to the hardworking and often discriminated foreign expatriates, "Man Yasma' Sauti" ("Who Listens to My Voice?") honestly presents a cruel aspect of Kuwaiti society that deserves more effort in finding solutions.

In the age of fighting terrorism, "Ishtibah" ("Resemblance") emits the fear of being a Musim who is an easy target of racial hatred or religious discrimination. The author was inspired by news articles about Muslim men being accused of terrorist activities ad therefore questioned whether or not their arrest and torture were simply because of their appearance and "suspicious" behavior—such as praying and congregating in mosques. Speaking through the male protagonist, Al Sanousi objects to that stereotyping of, and against, Arab Muslims. The protagonist laments that as a child life was much simpler, he did not have to be concerned with the complications he has had to face in adulthood and the simplistic labels others put on him. The protagonist believes a mosque to be a place where people listen to religious preaching and get closer to God. Unfortunately, the stereotype associating devout Muslims with terrorism has led innocent Muslims to false arrest and mistreatment.

---

[11] Al-'Uthman, "Yanfasil al-Watan... Tanfasil al-Tariq" ("The Nation Is Divided... The Road Is Divided"), *Carnet de Femme: Edition Bilingue*, Paris: UNESCO, 1997, pp. 261-9.

[12] Muna al-Shafi'i, "Akhir al-Masaat" ("The Last Evil Deed"), *al-Bayan*, no. 338 (September 1998), pp. 101-2.

[13] Wafa' al-Hamdan, "al-Daf' bil-'Umlah al-Sa'bah" ("Payment by Hard Currency"), *al-Tayaran bi-Janah Wahid* ("Flying with One Wing"), [Kuwait]: n.p., 1989, pp. 47-56.

Despite the fact that Al Sanousi's story may appear to be naïve or biased since it inevitably defends Muslims, Islam, and the role of Islamic schools and mosques, the author's cautioning discrimination again the Muslims and wish to live in peace should not be overlooked.

The story, "Alam bi-la 'Uyun" ("A World Without Eyes"), turns away from sensitive political and social issues to an author's struggle in literary creativity. Swinging between reality and imagination, the writer-protagonist is waiting for the moment of inspiration in which his characters and storyline would appear and take shape. As a creative writing workshop leader, Al Sanousi herself is intimately familiar with the writer's struggle. As she states,

> "'World without Eyes' is the world of the creative writer, as he is caught up in a world filled with characters, voices, scenes, and so forth. And they are all in an obscure place, where no one can see them except the creative writers who glimpse AT them as movie images within the darkness of his/her mind at the moment of inspiration. This world doesn't need eyes; it needs someone with talent who can visualize an animated world brimming with life and emotion. That world is without eyes. Creative writers can see via the faculties of their hearts and inspired minds."[14]

Al Sanousi's Kuwait

Al Sanousi's writings challenge the Western view on Kuwait. It is no longer simply an oil-rich nation that bears the accusations of mistreating its female citizens and foreign expatriates, or a society that cultivates clusters of Islamic fundamentalists and male chauvinists. It now presents a group of inhabitants who also have vulnerable feelings and fears, surrounded by a sea that plays many different and essential roles in their life. In Al Sanousi's stories readers find the full range of Kuwaiti voices and observe their everyday lives. Such aspects of Kuwait are never or rarely noticed elsewhere.

The author is also particularly concerned about the image of Kuwait presented in Arabic literature by Kuwaitis. On issues of women sexuality or victimization in the work of some Kuwaiti women writers, Al Sanousi provocatively states that "when anyone [especially from the West] reads their writings [i.e., those of some other Kuwaiti women writers], they might think that that is the face of Kuwaiti society and women's suffering. And I have to say directly: 'This is not true'."[15]

---

14 Haifa Al Sanousi, personal interview by mail, February 24, 2006.
15 Haifa Al Sanousi, personal interview by mail, February 24, 2006.

Her identification with her country is not shown through typically patriotic writings or in literature about war,[16] but by way of her in-depth and contentious observations of the strength of ordinary Kuwaitis in their everyday life, her highlighting of the values and principles of former days, as well as her belief in the positive aspect of Muslim life. In a real sense, she makes a robust attempt to do no less than correct and reestablish the identity of her nation.

As a Kuwaiti woman writer, Al Sanousi has shed new light on the image of a woman writer from the area. She does not hesitate to incorporate Islamic values and principles into her belief system and demonstrates that Western feminist ideology is not the only way to comprehend a woman's self-realization. Should Al Sanousi be considered an anti-feminist, or an "orthodox/religious feminist," i.e. one who attempts to embrace both religion and feminism? No matter which, if either, she certainly offers readers the opportunity to examine a Muslim society and Muslim women from an Arab and Islamic perspective. Ironically, in the West, Al Sanousi might be considered an "alternative voice" in contrast to Arab women such as Layla al-'Uthman, Nawal al-Saadawi, or Fatima Mernissi, who are better known there. Whether or not she represents a mainstream women's voice, she presents a different picture of Kuwait by her female subjectivity. One could even argue that she has reclaimed Islam by reincorporating women into society and religion and defining a new understanding of Arab feminism.

---

[16] After the first Gulf War, a number of Kuwaiti women wrote stories about war, which were considered the beginning of the Kuwaiti women's war literature. These writers include: Fatima Yusuf al-Ali, Thuraya al-Baqsami, and Muna al-Shafei. When asked why she did not write about similar subjects, Al Sanousi maintained that stories came to her mind, so it was not up to her to select the theme. But Al Sanousi did reveal that one of her forthcoming stories will deal with the impact of the Iraqi invasion in 1991.

Departure of the Sea

The surrounding walls just about suffocated me. Sharply, the odor of paint penetrated my nose. How I detested the odor of paint! I was used to the smell of houses built with mortar and the breeze of the sea. But such had vanished.

O, where were the mortared houses? Where was the *rahah*?[17] Where was the *rushanah*?[18] Where was the *jandal*?[19] Where was everything? All these things had vanished.

Where had my mother's face gone? That was another thing that had disappeared, without a trace.

Where had my father's face gone? Where was his pleasant voice chanting the Koran each dawn? Where was the sweetness of the calls for prayer that used to shake the walls of our home?

Where was my father's voice that woke us up every morning?

—Wake up, girls. It's time for prayer. Prayer is better than sleep.

Then my mother came repeating:

—Time for prayer. Hissah, Fissah, Nurah. Wake up and pray.

Hissah and I jumped up out of the bed to clean ourselves and pray, while Nurah still wrestled with her slumber.

My mother continued to nag until Nurah got up.

Where were those days? Gone already?

Yes. It appeared that they were gone and I would be leaving soon to live in another world, a world I had no clue of!

---

[17] *Raha* is a handmade grinder or hand-operated mill used in the past to grind crops.

[18] *Rushanah* is a kind of shelf the Kuwaitis used in the past to place items like incense and rosewater underneath a courtyard window.

[19] *Jandal* is a big tree twig that was used in the past by Kuwaitis for house construction. It was usually installed on the ceiling.

Time had left its traces on my body. Days drew wrinkles on my face. That was the judgment of destiny, which could never be reversed.

I looked at the ceiling of this room now. I looked out at a sky that I could barely see. My voice, submerged inside, was whispering religious expressions; these had never left me, not even for a single day. (O God, I pray for a gentle end.) That was a phrase whose spirit I inhaled in every corner of our old house.

While my tongue repeated it quietly, I felt as if I was breathing in the air of our house.

I was walking between the rooms. I saw the faces of my mother, father, and the faces of my sisters. I became a witness of the time that had gone.

I became a weak body carrying the features and memories of something called the sea. And was the sea that I saw years ago the same as the one my parents knew? No, no. I don't think so.

I felt a sudden shiver when the nurse opened the door of my room abruptly. I saw her carrying in her hands a container which had needles, alcohol, and other things whose names I hadn't the slightest idea of. She injected a needle into the vein of my right hand in order to withdraw a sample of my blood.

She then inserted into me another device.

I didn't protest. I never did. I didn't object at all. I surrendered to my fate completely.

I accepted this reality even though it was a bitter one. What was the use of protest? I endured the pain even as it hurt. I tried not to scream because I was used to suppressing my screams. Fate and destiny. One should not fight one's destiny.

A human was born and another died.

I was sorry for my children; they were taking turns visiting me and staying with me in my room when the nurse was not there.

Their eyes closely studied my face. They saw my weakness and were full of sorrow. I, in turn, felt their pain as well, but I was unable to change the situation. I was surrendering to the coming fate. The time for departure had arrived.

No use in fighting. No advantage to fight. I wished I had the ability to ease their internal pain. But I couldn't.

It hurt very much whenever the nurse injected that darn needle in my forearm. I started to loathe the moment when she walked in. I wished I could protest against what she was doing. I wished she could leave me to the mercy of the Creator.

The nurses had become exasperated with the adventure of searching for veins for injections. It seemed that my veins had already hurried off to leave me behind.

One agonizing prick followed another through this exhausting search, leaving behind a large bruise and causing me more pain. But still I was resistant.

I was accustomed to that resistance. Perseverance was my sole weapon in life.

I ached but I buried my voice as one who was used to burying her feelings since youth. I had lived and continued to live for others.

It was no use to complain and cry. Everything had become fruitless.

I was distressed when I observed the sad looks on my children. But fate did what it wished.

A discussion suddenly erupted among a group of doctors who failed to find an explanation for the sudden and frightening deterioration of my condition. An angry roar arose.

My children and grandchildren voiced their dissatisfaction regarding the doctors' failure.

I was observing everything around me. But I couldn't speak. It felt as if I was incapable of speaking. Or the words had been shut off inside and I couldn't let them out.

I felt I was in a different world lying between dream and reality. Sometimes I felt separated from the others because I had left for my big world, escaping from a small world that almost suffocated me.

Was the time for the final departure approaching? I wasn't sure but it seemed as if it was.

I heard the voice of one of my daughters. In deep distress, she was speaking to a doctor who was standing near my head and staring at me with a look that reprimanded me for still being alive at the age of eighty. He wished that I would hurry to depart so that he could put an end to the continuous concern and pressure in the questions he faced from my children every morning at the door of my hospital room.

I felt myself in a state of weakness such as I had never experienced before—a coma in which I had lost the ability to speak or even to listen to the conversations around me.

I was weak all over my body. There was something running in my veins that I couldn't identify. But I was convinced without a doubt that this thing was pushing me down into unconsciousness.

I mourned the predicament of my children, who stood near my head waiting for a sign of hope to emerge.

I didn't want to frustrate them but this weakness was devouring me, not allowing me any room to show the slightest strength of movement, not even a slight turning.

I had become like a sculpture with no power to move. But I kept whispering this expression: I will do my best not to torture myself nor anyone else.

One of my daughters would object whenever I repeated it in front of them. She thought it too early for such words.

—Death? Why are you talking about death, Mother?

—There is no escape from fate. Death is reality.

I saw the sadness on her face.

I was now in a situation I could not describe. I saw it and yet I didn't. I heard it and yet I didn't. Perhaps this was between life and death. I didn't know. But I proceeded toward the moment of departure. I would have to abandon my children like all other mothers. I wasn't the first and wouldn't be the last. Everyone has to leave. Everyone departs. It's only a matter of time.

Two nurses came more than once per day, to turn me.

I felt sad for myself, but I pushed the feeling down. I suppressed my fear as well. I feared the unknown that's coming and cannot be fought.

I was used to concealing my pain and sadness. I was used to concealing my internal worries and anxiety.

Usually I put a smile on my face in order for others not to feel what I felt. Today I couldn't even begin a smile. I didn't know if I could even make the effort. Or maybe I could no longer tell my facial expressions.

Another fright was assaulting me. I would sniff it in the room mixed within the stench of alcohol and medicine that I loathed.

The smile of my son Salih Sabah visited me everyday.

—Good morning, sweetest and most gentle mother in the world. How are you doing?

I wished I could respond. It was not that I couldn't respond at all, but there was something that held back my tongue and didn't allow me to give voice from deep inside. I was in a condition I couldn't explain.

Salih asked me again. His eagerness to hear my vanished voice in the past weeks almost tore him apart.

—I beg you, Mother, talk to me. Do you feel pain?

My long silence worried him. He found another way to communicate with my world.

—Can you understand me? Close your eyes if you can understand me.

I replied to him with an enthusiasm that was as minimal as the strength I had. His fear for me almost killed me. I used the only strength I had to communicate with this world as it seemed the time to say goodbye was fast approaching.

I closed my eyes again and then opened eagerly to see the impact of the response he wasn't expecting. I noticed the joy appearing on his face. I became happy, too. But I couldn't express even that simple happiness which sailed along the surface of my emotions.

Salih hugged me hard, so hard that he almost broke the bones that supported the thin layer of my wrinkled skin. He showered me with continual and warm kisses all over my face. He took my right hand, putting it on his heart. He kissed my hand deeply and then put it on his heart again.

I heard his heartbeat craving for my cure. His enthusiastic voice rose in my ears.

—By God's will, you'll recover, Mother. You'll come home. These are just simple tests. The whole thing will be over soon. You can leave this hospital and come back to us. You understand? I'll take you to the sea. You can put your feet in the water that you love so much. My wife Nuriyah can put some *henna*[20] on your hair and hide this gray. You'll be beautiful again like before.

The sea! A beautiful word had returned from a past that Salih knew nothing about.

I always loved the sea! I also always loved my youngest daughter Haya. Haya wished that the oil were gone so that we could return to the sea. She was another who knew nothing about the feel of the sea. But she longed for it and talked about it, as if she lived in it.

I couldn't forget her passion for life that touched me deeply. She left her tracks on the map of my body and mind.

—Mother, I wish the oil were finished. Then we could go back to the sea. We can put on *bakhnaq*.[21] We can wash our clothes in the sea. We can sleep right after the dinner prayer.

Haya brought me back to a past into which I had submerged myself for many years of my life. I felt as if my mother was talking to me gently in her bosom. I longed for the smell of my mother's *milfa'*.[22] I craved for my father's pleasant voice when he chanted the Koran. I missed the voice of my sister, Hissah, who had left me earlier for another world several years ago.

But would my daughter Haya have been satisfied with living in a house built with mortar near the mosque that my father built? Could she have endured the hardship of those innocent times that had passed long ago?

The call for prayer from the mosque still lingered in my memory. It would pierce my body and swamp me with warm feelings, facing down the anxieties that came upon me from time to time.

(God is the greatest. God is the greatest. I witness no gods but God. I witness Muhammad is the Messenger of God.) The call to prayer of the past remained. It penetrated the walls of our old house and lived on in my memory, joining now with Salih's voice, which kept reciting the prayer in my right ear.

The two voices intermingled and merged into one, one voice that united the past and the present, one voice that drove away the concerns and anxieties that shackled me from time to time. Perhaps Salih sensed my anxieties, so

---

[20] Henna is a plant. It is used as a dye, particularly in hair coloring, and temporary body art known as mehndi.

[21] Head shawl young girls used in the past.

[22] Head shawl Kuwaiti women used in the past.

he chased them away from deep inside of me. Poor Salih. He bore so many of my concerns.

Salih's comforting prayer filled my ear. Suddenly, his voice stopped. The old man's voice came, reading the Chapter of Al-Baqarah. A very pleasant and refined voice. But it didn't surpass the exquisiteness of my father's when he would chant the Koran in our house and in the mosque next door.

My children had been putting a tape recorder next to my head so that I could listen to some Koranic verses. They had learned my attachment to religion. They also had learned that my calmness came from the spiritual comfort.

My children were visiting me in the hospital. They were dying to find out if I could go home.

The doctors made more promises. Arrogant orders for my recovery had multiplied. Would I disappoint them if I passed away? I didn't know. It's a question to which I had no answer.

I felt a pressing desire to sleep. I closed my eyes and plunged into a deep sleep. Several people from the past visited me. I remembered my childhood, which I missed deeply.

I remembered my mother, father, and my sisters Hissah, Nurah, and Aishah.

My sister Hissah used to baby-sitting me for years. She then got married and left home. I missed her a lot because she had been very nice to me. I used to feel her heart very close to mine even though she was much older than I. As for my other sister Nurah, she was always energetic. We were close in age but she was always smarter than me in playing tricks.

Nurah had a quick temper and was spoiled in being allowed her own special world. Not only did she not assist my mother in doing housework, she even refused to obey her orders.

My poor mother was always troubled by Aishah's retardation and Nurah's extreme misbehavior.

—Nurah! Nurah!

My mother was calling Nurah.

—Nurah, where are you? Come quickly.

I was in the kitchen helping my mother cook lunch. Nurah was only two years younger than I, but she enjoyed life very much. She didn't miss any of the fun of childhood. She insisted on having fun at an early age. As for me, it felt like torture.

I was wise despite my youth. I did want to play with Nurah and her friends, but I pitied my mother who was continuously fulfilling her endless responsibilities. I felt it was necessary to help her with the burdens of the house.

—Darn that Nurah! She went off to play just like that. Fidhah, you are a sweetheart. Was I too harsh on you when I left you to bake bread? . . .

I interrupted her:

—No, no. I am happy to do this. I hope you stop repeating expressions like this. I feel very happy helping you. I also like to do the housework.

—But Nurah . . .

I interrupted her again:

—Nurah is still young. Let her play.

I hid my feelings and tried not to show my own strong desire to play with Nurah and her friends.

Nurah was playing right outside the door. She was having lots of fun. Her laughter and that of her friends flew inside. She herself was flying through the air on a swing that my dad built for us right by the door.

My mother continued to call:

—Nurah! Nurah!

—Leave her alone, Mother. Let her play.

—Don't you want to play!? How selfish she is. She should help me with some housework. She is no longer little. She will taste the fruit of her naughtiness.

Nurah became angry because of Mother's continuous imploring. She lost her balance, fell from the swing, and hit her face on the ground.

The screaming for help! The intense crying! The loud weeping was so powerful that it almost tore our mortar walls down.

Aishah came out from the room next to the kitchen. She looked at the scene with the innocence of a person who didn't know what to do with life. She came to us quickly, crying with a stammer that we had become accustomed to.

—N . . . u . . . u . . u . . . r . . . a . . . h . . . N . . . u . . . u . . u . . . u . . . r . . . a . . . h . . .

My mother read the frightened expression on Aishah' face. She jumped up anxiously and dropped the dough that her right hand was kneading.

—Fidhah. Fidhah. Your sister Nurah . . . something bad happened to her! Bring me my hair veil and face cover.

I rushed quickly to her room and grabbed the two items. She put them on and headed towards the door. I followed her closely.

We found Nurah covering her face with her hands, crying sorrowfully. The other little girls ran away as my mother arrived, fearing a scolding.

—My nose is broken! My nose is broken! It hurts badly.

Nurah was aching. But she would go on to survive the ordeal and become troublesome again later. I knew this. I was convinced of this.

We tried to remove her hands so that we could see her face. We were shocked by the big bulge around her nose. It would leave scars. Hopefully she would learn her lesson. My mother was disheartened. I immediately felt her heartbeat and the heaviness in her voice.

Nurah continued to scream. Then came my mother's trembling voice.

—In the name of God the Merciful and the Compassionate. May God protect you from Satan and all evils. Don't be frightened, my little one.

She quickly put her right hand on Nurah's head and started to recite some Koranic verses.

We helped carry Nurah into our room. Aishah gave us a strange look and started crying as well. She looked at my mother. Perhaps she was frightened.

—Fidhah. Bring a cup of water for your sister. Quickly before your dad comes back from the mosque. I am afraid that he would think I have been negligent.

I was very young at that time, but I was already carrying the responsibilities beyond my age. I was about twelve years old, but I was practicing the role of a mature woman.

I knew that I didn't enjoy my childhood. I deliberately avoided wearing children's clothes for the sake of my mother, because I empathized with her a lot. She changed after my sister Hissah's marriage. She felt bitter and isolated, but didn't show it.

I thought I had inherited some qualities from my mother. She didn't show her pain or emotions. The poor thing repressed every internal desire that breathed inside her in order to satisfy and please the others. I knew she was very sad every time she looked at my sister Aishah's face, part of which had been devoured by fire and had become disfigured.

Aishah continued to suffer from the huge disfigurement of her face and several spots on her body. It was fate: impossible to prevent or be on the alert for.

Poor Aishah was born disabled and suffered from an inborn defect in her right hand that had made it slightly paralyzed. In addition, she manifested imbecility since infancy. Fate almost snatched her away when one day the kitchen caught fire and she nearly died. Then a miracle happened. But the fire still had left scars on her face and body.

I was in pain when I perceived the grief on my mother's rigid face and in her voice, which seemed inaudible most of the time. She recalled my brother Ahmad who died in infancy. Her heart was broken at his death. He was her only son. She was hoping to have another boy.

—Fidhah, take care of your sister Aishah, if I die.

I put my hand on her lips. Tears in my throat almost smothered me. I gave her a big hug. Tears gushed onto my cheeks.

—May God relieve your poor sister Aishah. Paralyzed, burned, and retarded. Everything is on her. I ask God forgiveness. I ask God forgiveness. Praise be to God, no one protects the detestable except Him.

My unfortunate mother. She was exhausted from cooking and caring for all the children, and carrying out the demands of her husband, cleaning the house, washing clothes, etc., in addition to the intense and constant care my sister needed. There were also loads of other responsibilities. May God give her rest.

Praise be to my father, who had departed earlier.

—Fatimah. Fatimah. Where are you?

My mother left her room and headed toward my dad.

—You came back early today.

—I did the midday prayer. Then I suddenly felt tired. The sun is harsh and my headache hasn't left me since early this morning.

—Peace be with you. Peace a thousand times. Should I prepare lunch?

—Yes.

My mother hurried to the kitchen with me following her. She didn't know that I was ahead of her and had lunch ready.

—Fidhah. Nurah. Aishah. Your father is back from the mosque.

She turned to me suddenly looking at me with pride, out of which I knew she recognized my existence.

—Sweetheart, I hope God will bestow upon you a well-behaved son soon who will pamper you, because you deserve it.

I was disturbed by her plea, because she was a wonderful mother and I didn't want to leave her.

—A well-behaved son who would pamper me? Nothing is stopping me, but not now. I am still young.

She took a big spoon and scooped rice from the pot.

—Young?

She smiled looking at me and said:

—O Fidhah, you have already grown up. You should know that you'd get married soon. Marriage is a protection for girls. Then . . .

I interrupted her:

—I beg you, Mother, not to talk about this subject now. Please, not now.

She gave me a smile that cheered me up again and made me forget the horrifying accident that had been stressing me for a while.

We turned to the table. Aishah came, with Nurah following her. Father turned to Nurah to examine her carefully. We all noticed the anger emanating from his eyes. My mother came quickly.

—What's wrong? Is something bothering you?

My father didn't answer but kept looking at Nurah's face. Nurah was confused. She kept holding back her breath. I entered the crisis:

—What happened, Father?

—Nurah. You are wearing *diram*?[23] Why are you wearing it, you mischievous little girl?

---

[23] Diram: Kuwaiti women used it to color their lips in the old time.

Nurah stared at the ground. We all plunged into this moment of silence. Only Aishah continued to eat greedily.

—Did you go to sister Maryam's house?

Nurah remained silent. Mother replied:

—Fidhah did. We should bless her soon for her reciting the Koran. She now knows how to read and write. Fidhah makes us pleased.

My father's anger turned to be a gentle smile as Nurah's face was just turning frightened. We exchanged looks.

Aishah interrupted the silence with a broken expression that was hard to understand:

—D . . . i . . . r . . . a . . . m . . . N . . . u . . . r . . . a . . . h . . .

All became still. Mother jumped in:

—The *diram*'s color will disappear after a few days. Don't do it again, Nurah. I warn you.

Nurah swallowed a mouthful of food together with her fear of my father.

Childhood years passed quickly. I turned fourteen years old.

One day, after my father returned from his Friday prayer, we had lunch as usual. My father turned to my mother, whispering in her ears something that I could hear.

—I want to discuss with you something, Umm Ahmad.

—As God wills it.

He left the room. She followed and closed the door. After an hour, my mother came to our room.

—Fidhah. It seems that my prayer has come true. It hasn't been long.

—What?

—Abu Ibrahim came to ask for your hand.

—Who? Abu Ibrahim? I will marry him?

—He is conservative and balanced, unlike thoughtless young men. His wife died last year. They have several children.

—Mother, I am still young. Why are you in a hurry to marry me off?

—Listen, Fidhah. You will get married sooner or later. Abu Ibrahim is a good man. Your father has seen the piety and religiousness in him.

—Mother, I know that, but . . .

—Trust God, my daughter. God will take care of you. You will have my blessing.

A strange and scary sensation that I had never experienced before carried me away.

—Do I have to leave our home, Mother? Do I need to leave here? I am scared. Very scared.

My body was trembling all over. My mother understood my fear, so she hugged me tight. I felt unusual warmth deeply surrounding me. It was just like my first time feeling her bosom. I wanted to see my sister Hissah.

—Will I be able to see Hissah before marriage? I would like to see her, Mother. She should know. It's impossible that . . .

An enormous fear came to me.

—My sweetheart, she will know. Of course, she'll know. I'll send our neighbor, Umm Mansur, to see her. I'll ask her to visit us the end of this week. I'll let your father know that you have agreed. He'll be happy about this. You know he loves you very much.

My voice cracked:

—I agree. I agree, Mother. I trust Father's opinion and choice.

I went to my room. Aishah was playing with a doll made of clothes. She was in another world. As for Nurah, she was asleep. Fear started to crawl all over my body. Was it true that I had to leave my father's house? Would I have to live in another home? I didn't know what my fate was going to be. I felt that this house was waiting for a new event, my marriage arrangement. I would move to a new home, a new home.

Then it all happened. I was so scared when I moved to the new house. I left my father's home. I could no longer see my mother's beautiful face everyday. I felt estranged in my husband's home. I didn't adjust easily. The walls of the house formed a cage that imprisoned me. I couldn't go out. Sometimes I felt suffocated. I felt the need for my mother's bosom. I needed her. I wished I could talk to her. I was in need of her hugs.

Abu Ibrahim was nice and considerate. But his mother was a mean and stubborn lady, who stared at me with rage and didn't tolerate the fact that I was a young child. She clearly despised me. I was trying different ways to please her; I tried ever so hard to get a look of acceptance from her. But she didn't think I was mature. She complained about everything, made fun of my cooking, and laughed at all my attempts to take care of my husband.

She wasn't satisfied with me at all. Perhaps she underrated me for my young age. She considered my youth a sign of weakness that should be rejected. She knew that Ibrahim, the son of my husband, was about my age.

I wanted to prove to her the opposite. I didn't want her to complain to my mother and my husband. I wanted to prove to my mother and my husband that I was a mature woman and that I was ahead of my actual age and I had already crossed the boundary of my childhood, which I looked down upon and hadn't found enjoyable.

I couldn't complain about her unfairness to my husband and my mother. My suffering was shackled deep inside me. I didn't want to hurt their feelings. I highly respected the kindness of their hearts and therefore wouldn't do anything to harm them.

I knew my husband loved me very much. He was happy with our marriage. I was young and beautiful, quiet and poised. I had become mature early. Abu

Ibrahim appreciated me a lot in that respect. He always praised me where we were alone away from his mother.

One day he came back from work after the noontime prayer, his mother was ready to cause problems. The conversation started:

—I am going to send her back to her father. She is of no use to you. You have married a baby. She doesn't listen to my advice.

He kissed her on her forehead, with a smile appearing on his gentle face.

—It's only a matter of time, Mother. Give her another opportunity.

She turned to him and raised her voice:

—Those who don't obey are lost. She can't bear any responsibility. This girl doesn't suit you.

He kissed her forehead again and smiled.

—Mother, I hope you can give her another opportunity. Fidhah has extraordinary morals. Her father is a sheikh of faith and a man of piety.

She interrupted him harshly:

—Your words are not true. There are plenty of other girls. What you found is a child.

He held her hand, kissed it, and put it on his chest.

—Mother, please. Fidhah likes you a lot. She always talks about you . . .

She withdrew her hand with force. She stood there with difficulty. She turned her back and headed back to her room repeating:

—I am not a child so don't mock me with petty expressions like this. We took her from her father's house to raise her. Misfortune . . . Misfortune . . .

She closed the door of her room forcefully. A sign of the end of the conversation.

I saw from a distance the trace of sadness on his face, but there was nothing to be done. I quickly closed the door so that he wouldn't feel that I was listening and that I had already jotted down this painful discovery in my memory.

He gently opened the door and found me sitting on the bed pretending to be busy sewing his *dashdasha*[24] that needed to be fixed. He kissed my cheeks. I gave him a smile, behind which were a hidden sadness and anxiety.

—How are you, Fidhah?

—I am fine. Thank God.

I put the *dashdasha* on the bed.

—I'll prepare lunch for you.

He held my hands gently with one hand and put the other on my dark hair.

---

[24] Robe-like garment men wear in Kuwait and much of the Middle East.

—Fidhah, you see.

He looked at me with love, smiling. How I loved his smile. It was a kind fatherly smile that I needed a lot after leaving my father's home.

—How beautiful you are! How gentle you are! Do you know that, Fidhah? God has already compensated me after the death of the kind Umm Ibrahim. I felt so lonely, but fate brought you into this house so that I forgot my concerns. You have filled my life, Fidhah. I almost forgot Umm Ibrahim. Can you believe that? Me, forgetting Umm Ibrahim?

I smiled, indulged in enormous joy. At this special loving moment, I tasted something that I had never felt before. That day I felt the need of a moment like this, which would nurture my emotions after separating from my mother. I didn't know what to say. All I knew was that I leaned toward him. But was this love? The same kind of love understood by people today? I didn't know. I didn't know. All I knew was that I was happy every time he came home and I became sad when he was ill.

The only person disturbed by my happiness was his mother, who never accepted my existence in that house.

I was craving a visit to my mother, but I feared my mother-in-law.

—Is it possible to visit my home today? It's been many weeks and I miss seeing my parents.

He gave me a smile as usual, a mesmerizing one.

—Of course, Fidhah. You can go.

I only lived with him for two years. He died from a terrible heart attack. He left me while I was still very young. However, he left me with a beautiful daughter, who resembled him a great deal.

I couldn't imagine myself alone in that house with his mother. Fate decided that death would creep again into the house and snatch away my mother-in-law only a few months after his death. This incident was a strong proof to me that it was time to return to my father's home. A young widow, who wasn't older than sixteen years of age.

My daughter Sara filled my life. I always watched her with new feelings that consumed my emotions. She gave me confidence again. I learned about motherhood at early age. Sara wasn't just a baby doll; she was alive.

I went back to my old room. I slept near my sister Aishah's bed. As for Nurah, she had gotten married to a man who lived in a district far away from us. We saw her once a month.

I didn't know that I would live a new life only a little less than a year after the death of my husband. But fate always has different events planned for us everyday. Another man knocked on the door of my life. I was afraid of another marriage because of Sara. I was hoping my future life would be successful, my husband would be nice, like my first husband.

—Fidhah, you should get married again.

My mother said, with a beautiful smile on her face mixed with signs of pressure and fatigue.

—I am concerned about Sara.

She interrupted me:

—Don't be. No other men are better than this one. He is very nice. Your father praises him a lot. Not to worry. I will ask God to help you. You are a nice woman. Nice men are for nice women.

I entered into a new life but with worry always following me. Still I found the man to be as nice as my father had said. I started to feel more relaxed and my body was no longer tense.

Years passed. I gave birth to one boy after another. My life was accompanied by the screaming and crying of babies who crawled, stumbled in learning to walk, and got into fights with neighbors' children.

My life was very exhausting, but was surrounded with love that filled my lungs with fresh air. I lost Sara when she moved to her husband's house and left me alone with six babies. They now have grown up and gotten married. I became a grandmother with many grandchildren.

I was ready to live my new life, except that the sea wouldn't leave my memory. It remained with me. It settled deep inside of me.

I looked out at the room again. I saw the face of the Filipina nurse, who was giving me a shot. I no longer felt the pain. I felt that I didn't have enough power to even keep open my eyes. I wanted to say farewell to my children with one quick glance. I wanted to see their faces one last time.

The time had come. Now was the time to depart. I felt weaker and weaker. The faces of my father, mother, sister Hissah, my former husband, and others had come back to me. The house built with mortar returned. The mosque's prayer started to be chanted: (God is the greatest. God is the greatest. God is the greatest. I witness no gods but God.)

I took my last breath and felt strangled.

I saw a bundle of light, heading toward me, taking away my vision. My tongue grew very heavy . . .

*　　*　　*

A World Without Eyes

From the Notes of A Fiction Writer

Birth

I sat down to write something.
There are summons here and there.
From people close enough for me to see clearly
And people so far away that I can't tell their facial features.
I feel an extreme thirst and a strange connection to one of these people.
I know now what I am doing. Yes, I know
That I am weaving new storylines for which I haven't chosen a name yet.
Perhaps because I haven't yet finished the story.
Or perhaps because I have yet to start.
Some thoughts are dropped from my mind. One after another.

Throttling

I try to collect them again. Some have slipped through and I can't grab them. I can't
I feel a strong tension,
Which almost strangles me.
Finally,
A star is born in a place outside my mind.
It has come to bury the dark that wants to expand in my home.
But the star . . .
It appears the star is lost. It doesn't know its way. Or perhaps the star is mute and can't express what it wants.
My youngest child's scream disturbs me.

His cry obscures many things.
Is it possible that he'll stop screaming?
I find myself saying:
(Silence. I need silence so that I can write. So that I can write.)
The storylines have scattered.
An attempt to finish it.

A Cup of Tea

I try to recover what may be rescued.
My heart is sad. It has flown away. One thought was born and has flown away
To the sky that is impossible to reach.
I shout in order to get rid of some of my tension.
(Aminah. A cup of tea without sugar. Quickly, please.)
I haven't recognized the picture buried inside me.
A noisy and lively city. Colors. Dense movements. Light. Darkness. Light. Darkness.
I am woken up from my world by the voice of my wife Aminah.
(Tea, my love)
She closes the door of my office and has left after greeting me with a smile that I know every detail of.
How can I recover the thoughts that have been lost?
How can I gather the storylines again?
I look for the faces of these thoughts that are hiding.
I try to search for the wings they use to fly

Bullets of Death

I don't want to lament for her
No. She hasn't died.
She hasn't died.
Has she?
I will doze off in my chair. I will lean my head to the back. I will close my eyes.
Perhaps I will see her ghost so that I can hunt her down again.
Am I hunting her down or is she hunting me?
I don't know.
O I remember now.
It is jealousy.

The jealousy of Sulayman, my colleague at work. He has sprayed the picture of my stories with many bullets of death from afar.

He always asks me:

—How do you become a famous writer? Is it possible for me to become one like you?

I say:

—Writing is a gift. Something is born alongside a person like a twin. It is impossible to acquire it.

He replies jokingly:

—Do you think yourself as a philosopher? Are you trying to make me believe that you are ingenious and we are stupid? Are you inventing impossible scenarios?

I concentrate a little.

I am wondering. I am disappearing in the void of the dark

I can no longer see colors. I no longer hear sound.

Where is the picture in my memory?

Rain

I am dozing off.

I see a strange moment between reality and dream.

Rain is coming down.

I find myself in a desert that doesn't know the taste of the rain.

And I decide to build my city there.

I will plant my seeds there. And I will water them with my tears.

I will let them hear the melody of my sorrow and happiness.

I will wet the sand with water.

I will pray humbly to God so that stars will lighten up the gloom of the desert and the rain will come.

I see a wing. I see the moon.

I hear sounds. I see colors.

Here is my hero coming from the remote void.

He mounts on a horse.

I hear his voice rising.

I see the green oasis.

Where is the desert?

The rain is ample. He has found his way to my city.

I open my eyes.

I write

And write.

I put down the pen.
The title expands:
(A world without eyes.)
I hear my youngest's crying again.
I smile this time:
(Aminah. Aminah. Come and bring with you that little darn Khalid.)

*   *   *

Delusions

Awatif was a very ordinary woman. She spent most of her life taking classes. Schools, training courses, and workshops. She didn't remember most of what she learned at school, finishing with only a diploma in arts at the end of the program of study. Such trouble to get a low grade but it almost allowed her to enter a special arts program that accepted only underachievers. As soon as she received her diploma, she got married to a man who was ordinary, just like herself. He often contrasted himself with her because of his college degree, and his loud and powerful voice that just about shook down the walls of the house. It pleased him to always accuse her of a stupidity that he saw mixed with delusions. She was distressed everyday because of his continuous sharp criticism which she would receive for a variety of reasons.

When she had had a sickly child, she was sure her husband was going to repeat the following speech in her ears everyday:

—You don't have luck in anything. No college degree. No jobs. I don't even think you can give birth to a healthy baby in the future.

She was very frightened by the reality in which she lived and the unknown future awaiting her with this man. The retarded baby who was already two years old reminded her of her lack of success in many areas: her failure in school, which then prevented her from getting a nice job, and so on.

When she thought about getting rid of anxiety by going to work, she could not find any respectable job except for one in a center for people with disabilities. The wage was minimal.

She kept on thinking, but fear and delusion were coming together inside of her: a retarded baby at home and retarded people at work. No. No . . . She screamed from inside, voicing her protests.

She spent her time watching daily soap operas and became addicted to the plots of romantic films. Love, marriage and the happy ending.

She lived inside this beautiful dream, but then returned to her reality, continuing to bear her distress. She submerged her soul into the running of

41

a long race in which she couldn't catch her breath. Hope wouldn't allow her to achieve any goal, anything respectable. Delusions attacked her and she wasn't able to fight back.

Her husband's roar in the morning and evening brought the delusion deeper inside her and dug its claws in.

Was it fear or yet another delusion? She wasn't able to tell the difference any more.

Had her continuous thoughts of anxiety driven her into a state of paralysis?

—Look at yourself. Face the bitter reality. People don't respect you.
What fool would give you a respectful look?

Such upsetting words continued to sear her nerves.

She wished to return to the past, to the day when her mother supported her decision to marry this deluded man, who always bragged about his college degree while she had returned to high school a second time and failed to receive a diploma to enter a college. Why did he marry her? For her beauty? Yes. That was her only strong point. Her features drew attention and turned people's eyes. But who knew that she carried a soul struggling with delusions, which menaced her well-being?

Conversations started normally with a self-aggrandizing introduction:

—I choose friends carefully.

She looked at him with rage. He placed a big piece of grilled chicken in his mouth. Almost choked. Coughing. His face turned red and redder. He became congested. She was confused, but quickly brought a glass of water. He took a small sip, then took a deep breath. He was back to normal.

—Stupid! You can never behave well. A soulless bimbo.

He shuddered and left the room. He then remembered something that he wanted to tell her. He returned angrily.

—I have a meeting at five o'clock. Don't forget to wake me up one hour before the appointment.

She became very nervous. Her jaws froze. She took a glass of water and sipped. She then took a deep breath.

She didn't love him. She couldn't even bear the sight of his face. But she remained respectful. Respect, a word her ears were so used to hear from her mother. (Maintaining respect keeps a marital relationship in a good shape.) Her mother often repeated that phrase.

Good shape? So what the heck was it that tore her up everyday? She had become a sculpture owned by a mad artist.

Fear overcame her, followed by delusions and then impotence. Somewhere there was a cry hidden deep down that sought to breathe fresh air but couldn't reach out.

She turned on the television, put in a videotape, and started watching the remaining film. The conversation between the two stars of the film went like this:

—How beautiful you are!

—You are so handsome.

A spicy hug between newlyweds . . . The hug emitted the fire, respect, and warmth that she craved. She uttered a sigh from the bottom of her heart, but that was done completely in silence. She dozed off on the sofa. Stretching her legs and surrounded by the voice of the heroine in the film, she noted it in her journal and repeated the notations in a loud voice.

She was alive in this moment; her being expanded.

Something powerful extended from her rose blossom dreams and into the green earth. She immersed herself in it and felt warmth.

Sadness returned. That foolish man controlled everything in this house, even the temperature of the air conditioner. He preferred cold; she preferred warmth, but couldn't have it. He deprived her of everything. Delusions came, and became her companion. But these impossible dreams always gave way to cruel reality. Was it possible to stop hallucinating?

One day he spoke to her angrily:

—You are not allowed to keep this servant any more. Not even one more day.

—Why? I need her . . .

—She doesn't say a word. You don't have any emotion. The two of you live in numbness.

—We should have a discussion about this issue of sending the servant back to the office. The issue . . .

He interrupted her, rudely:

—What? Now you are challenging my decisions? That's bizarre! You challenge me on things that you know nothing about? I am the decision-maker here. As for you, your life is very limited.

—My God! What have you done to this poor thing? I beg you to give her another opportunity. She didn't understand your request.

—Enough from you. Tell her to pack her bags. In two hours, she will return to the laborers' office. I gave you an opportunity to pick a servant and what was the result? Failure. Does it make sense that I live with a second dimwit?

She suddenly had a terrible headache. She felt frozen in this cold moment. He went on his way and she went on hers.

Lying on the sofa, she turned on the video and started watching the same film, the same section. She plunged into the warm moment, an iceberg in her chest started to melt. Part of the dream scattered, the same dream that wouldn't leave her alone.

Perhaps the servant was just today's scapegoat. She was imprisoned forever in the walls of this gloomy house. She would become the only scapegoat everyday and live at the mercy of an unknown fate.

She had brought respect into the house, as her mother advised. Wasn't it possible for her to enjoy it as well? She remembered her mother's soft voice. She shouldn't disappoint her. She should continue to endure this daily nightmare. She should continue this journey. But then there was something else important, which was the daily scream concealed behind a heart passionate only about her beauty.

She also remembered a workshop she attended entitled "How to Become a Successful Wife" and another workshop called "The Art of Interacting with Self and Others." She attended them upon her cousin's strong urging. She never finished the workshops.

One paragraph written in her notes remained in her memory, which the lecturer repeated frequently: "We are equipped with psychological tools that generate desires, which help us go through hard times. We are the ones who create dreams. We are also the ones who choose our roads to failure or empowerment."

She quickly walked to the bedroom and looked at her face in the mirror. She put some makeup on after having stopped doing so for more than a year. She needed to feel like a woman who was alive within. She smiled because she saw in the mirror a man who was unable to read but was passionate when looking at her. She hid the smile and put back on her usual face. The road ahead now was going to be long and hard.

*   *   *

Escape

The announcement repeats over and over: "Attention please. The airlines announce that . . . about the departure flight number . . . destination . . ."

He is walking with heavy steps, carrying a small piece of luggage in his right hand and a teacup in the other which contains the kind of tea he is used to drinking each morning. But today he is drinking the tea at the airport's café, ready to leave the refuge where he had done his best to remove the intense feelings pressed upon him by events in life.

This time he decided to spend a few weeks, not just a few days as he always did. He wanted to stay away from a tragedy that almost blows his life away.

He asks himself . . . Is escape the best solution to my dilemma? No. No. I don't think so. But I am not able to face it. I can no longer endure it. I can't face this weak creature that has lived inside me for many years. I have tried to get rid of this thing that has now more or less overtaken me. Its spider-like web wraps around me and destroys my soul and stops me from breathing.

Is it going to stay inside me for long? I want to strip it from me and have it find a way out. It overpowers me and accompanies me everywhere. People look at me and point at me because I am defeated all the time under these overpowering circumstances. Yes, I am defeated. I'm not strong enough to face the sneering looks that freeze me with their whips. I can't even defend myself.

Is it possible for me to change? No, I can't because I have tried many times. I read many books about improving personality. Nothing has changed. In the meantime, I am living with something that has been dwelling inside me for many years. What's the solution? How do I escape from the situation I am in? Perhaps this can't happen unless my exhausted soul leaves the scrawny body that isn't able to bear me from place to place. A strange feeling has come and penetrates me.

Loneliness is my companion on the road. An ambiguous question keeps harassing me and demands an answer. But I can't do anything about it. The question repeats like an echo. The pain becomes stronger, while the thought of escape has come to me. But what kind of escape? I don't know how this vision began to distract me and dominate most of my thought. I begin to feel hesitant, but can't find an interpretation for it.

I took my friend's advice to take a medical exam. As the appointment was approaching, my body started to show some symptoms. I weakly submitted to every exam, but they found nothing. Nothing. The loathsome x-ray even penetrated my body and my head to seek out the reasons for the symptoms that bothered me.

Anxiety started to attack me constantly and even became part of me. The result had always been defeat, that is, I was always defeated. That was the result I had for every situation I have been in for all my life.

I finally decided to fight with the self-esteem that came to me from time to time. I decided to visit my psychologist because I found myself in need of tranquilizers to kill the screams of pain that were voiced inside me and defeated me all the time. I wanted to taste the relaxation that I was forbidden. I wanted to feel independent after these psychological crises in my life out of which I always emerged weaker. I was tormented because I was unable to find the answer to the embarrassing question that kept echoing in my head.

My first marriage ended with failure. My second marriage was crowned with flagrant adultery. My wife was unable to give me love, because she just never loved me. She was forced to accept me as a husband so that she could cut off the previous relationship that didn't satisfy her family. I was the victim of adultery. One day I discovered that she was talking to a man and revealed her love to him and her disgust toward me.

She succeeded in commanding my life and taking control of my decisions. I was submissive to her because I didn't want to fail in my second marriage. But ultimate tragedy continued to travel alongside me throughout my life.

She enjoyed her own beauty, which would turn people's eyes, accompanied by a sweet voice no one could resist. In spite of the accumulated sadness that I suffered deep inside, I was attached to her. I felt I was attracted to her. But she hurt me with a surprise betrayal of our marriage and then called me foolish when I confronted her with the truth of her deeds. She was very harsh in her words. I couldn't to let go of that sin.

I remembered the day when I left her. I wished I could strangle her, but I didn't have the courage to do so. That creature living inside me paralyzed my ability to revenge.

I didn't carry on like a miserable child, but I felt something hidden inside, which caused me suffering and turned my life upside down immediately afterward. That sense of crisis has attacked again, turning my life into hell. I have finally realized that every crisis that I thought would be the last is never the last.

*　　*　　*

Resemblance

—What is your name?

—It should be recorded in your log. Sharp anger rose. The tone of voice became higher.

—I know that. But you should answer my question. Do you understand? He raised his head angrily. He remembered that he should be submissive and obedient, as his sister advised.

—Abd al-Rahman al- . . .

—How old are you?

—Thirty.

—Married or single?

—Married with one daughter only.

—What do you do?

—I'm a teacher of Islamic education.

—Since when?

—Since five years ago.

—And your previous job?

—I used to work as an assistant to an office manager before that. I mean, when I was a student at a university. I studied in the morning and worked in the evening.

—What's your relationship to this incident?

—I don't have anything to do with it. The investigator grabbed the edge of his beard with a hand and suddenly spoke coldly:

—It looks as if you are better off having nothing to do with it. He was upset, moving in the small narrow space on a chair that couldn't hold his heavy body.

—I will talk to the judge. Where is the judge who . . .

—Quiet! You listen and answer my questions only. What do you know about those individuals who plotted the explosion? He smiled and remained silent. A wave of anger surged again. Then a sudden shout.

—I will teach you a lesson you will never forget. I can promise you that. He called over the police.

—Take this guy and put him in isolation. He walked in heavy steps. Along came deep anxiety. He remembered his beard, which made everyone look alike everywhere.

He couldn't forget some of the expressions he heard when sometimes he was compelled to accompany his wife to the market after being strongly pressed by her. She couldn't move her eyesight from those girls who wore very tight clothes and put perfume that stretched for miles.

He was put in solitary confinement. He lay down on his back, staring at the ceiling.

He realized his predicament. Several people visited him.

My situation is bad. My childhood was very beautiful. I wouldn't have even thought of the outcome of the current situation. I wouldn't have been concerned about what happened outside me. My world was about me only. A child's world is a child's world. All they were concerned about was not playing enough. At the end of the day, I slept without worries. I had beautiful dreams and colorful fantasies. The only concern I began to have was about school—examinations and the physical education teacher. He was very serious and didn't explain the subject conscientiously. I had to avoid enrolling in the music class especially after the mosque's preacher nearby our house told us that music was forbidden and that I should stay away from listening to it. Why were my worries so simple but have no grown so large Why have I become an object of suspicion?

My grandfather was known for his piety. He used to stay in the mosque more often than at home. Nothing happened to him. People were blessed by his prayer and rushed to attend his religious lecture. What happened to the world?

Seconds passed like hours. He was told by a thin policeman wearing a smile that he was bailed out.

—Thank God. Your picture is not published in the newspaper.

He remained silent. Words became tinged with anxiety. But how was he bailed out? There was a need to know the answer.

He remembered his cousin who married the daughter of a local representative. It must have been him who solved the problem. But suspicions caused by resemblance . . . were they going to end?

*   *   *

Waiting

He looked at the clock hanging on the opposite wall, feeling tired from sitting on the chair for a long time. All of a sudden, he jumped up with all his energy and walked toward the nurse who had opened the doctor's door and called out the name of the next patient.

He approached her and noticed that she was getting nervous. He kept his eyes on the sign of agitation on her face. He spoke in a choked voice because of the backache that had intensified a week ago.

—Could you make sure that my file is with the doctor? I have been here since seven o'clock.

She paid him no attention and cut off his words by a holler that almost tore his left eardrum.

—Khalid Abd Allah. Khalid Abd Allah.

Here came Khalid Abd Allah. She went in with him and then decided to lock the door with a key. He felt defeated, weak; his backache worsened as he grew upset. He looked at the faces of other patients. Then he moved his eyes to the chair where he had been sitting for more than two hours. He saw an elderly woman with a cane, sitting in his place. What could he do? Should he continue to stand? What about his backache? He was supposed to endure it. There was no other solution. He had to be in this waiting room.

He leaned against the wall. Several seconds passed. The pain intensified. So did the throbbing twinge on his back. The unnatural movement of his right knee indicated that his legs were about to collapse. He forgot this morning to put on some ointment that his daughter Fawziyah's girlfriend brought from London.

His knee was addicted to the ointment. It was important to reduce the pain that reinforced the slow pace of time's passing, and the approach of the End, which just added more anxiety. An interior voice repeated:

—Praise be to God, who doesn't give bad things to people.

He broke the silence and started to talk. He uttered a sentence from deep inside that his tongue wouldn't stop repeating:

—There is no god but God. Muhammad is the messenger of God.

The pain intensified. It was no longer limited to his back only. It had spread to his right knee as well.

He could no longer stand. He felt like collapsing. He remembered the angry nurse who had added another element that worsened his continuing complaint. She didn't care about the feelings of the patients. And she knew that there was no punishment and that patients had no one to complain to.

—My God. The country is no longer ours. And the people have also changed.

He tried to grab the attention of a young man sitting next to him. The young man turned and said:

—Please sit down . . .

He stood up before completing his phrase.

—Please, sir . . . .

Abu Nasir continued to talk, feeling the exhaustion that covered every corner of this waiting room.

—My back has been aching for a week. So painful I couldn't stand it. My right knee is used to the ointment that my daughter's friend brought from London. I forgot to put it on today.

—Don't look at the dark side. Peace be with you. The young man leaned on the wall and gave Abu Nasir a gentle smile.

Abu Nasir put his hand on his knee trying to squeeze the painful area. The pain even gripped his heart, but his hand wasn't able to apply any force. He stared at a hand that already betrayed the marks of time.

Some days are for you and some days are against you.

He recalled that expression Fawziyah liked to say.

—You have become too skinny, Dad. I have to take care of your diet.

He had remained at home for more than a year without going out after the death of his wife. He then listened to the urgings of his daughter Fawziyah, who pointed out that it was necessary to change the routine of his life. He started visiting the café near the shore. There were old men chatting all night, flipping old newspapers. He watched them talking inside some mortar houses. He inhaled the ocean breeze and walked to the Qublah quarter.

Memory came alive at the café. There in the Qublah quarter was the sound of the call for prayer from Ali Bin Himd Moqsue. He used to pray in the mosque at dawn and not go back to bed afterward. He came to the café daily. The café became a new cradle for his old memories. There were hard days, but with beautiful memories.

The nurse came out again. Her face grew more irritated. He tried to keep his eyes away from her in order not to see her gloomy expression.

He looked at the clock on the wall. 10:00 am. He mumbled to himself.

—May God help her, if God's wills.

The nurse opened her mouth to shout as usual. It showed that her teeth were stained by the glaring red lipstick that she was wearing.

—Habib Khan. Habib Khan. A young South Asian man with dark skin approached, dragging a very skinny body.

The nurse grew angrier as she saw him, not even a little mercy for his weakness. She raised her voice saying:

—Hurry up. Hurry up. They entered the doctor's room. She appeared totally irritated.

Abu Nasir grumbled. Anger and tiredness from waiting made him very upset. A phrase got stuck in his head that he couldn't get rid of. He looked to the right muttering:

—God Almighty. We have become strangers. This homeland is our ancestors' . . .

He held back the rest of the sentence as he saw the face of a stranger sitting next to him.

He remembered being at home alone. The home had two floors, locating in the suburb of Abd Allah Al-Salim. The house had lost life and was surrounded by silence and darkness. There was no light in the house except his room, which had become a bedroom, a dining room, and a living room. The house became deserted after Fawziyah's marriage and Nasir's departure with his wife and children to America to obtain a master's degree. The house became even more deserted after his wife left for another world. A departure with no return.

He looked again at the guy's angry face and mumbled to himself: (Thank God I didn't finish the sentence. I should take caution. He could have retaliated against me. I don't want to be killed. Our neighbor Abu Saud's incident shocked me. Newspapers reported extensively about it for the whole week. His Asian servant killed him for his money. His children abandoned him and left him at the mercy of an Asian servant who didn't know one word in Arabic.

Abu Saud died of suffocation. The wealth ended up with his children who didn't cry much over their father's death. He had been very greedy. God have mercy on him. Poor Abu Saud died bereaved. Killed. He was strangled with pillow. No. No. I can't die of strangulation. I'd better keep quiet.)

His cell phone rang. He took the phone out from the right pocket. He didn't forget Fawziyah's advice: Father, make sure to put your cell phone in the left pocket of your dashdasha. I am afraid that it will affect your heartbeat. Don't forget that a pacemaker is implanted in your heart. Cell phone frequency can affect that.

—How are you today?

—I am fine, my daughter. Thank God for everything.

—Are you still waiting?

—Yes and I can't do anything.

—But now it's already ten o'clock and you've been there since seven. What's with this mess? I told you a specialized hospital is better. I hope God allows you to listen to others. You thought your opinion was best. He interrupted her:

—Don't worry about me, sweetheart. It will be my turn soon, God willing. God is merciful, my daughter. I look forward to your visit tomorrow. Don't forget to buy some toys that Fawaz asked me for.

—As God wills. Bye.

—Bye.

He took a deep breath and remembered Umm Nasir, who went through a great deal of agony before death. She was very weak and could no longer move the right side of her body. He was very concerned because she hadn't been able to walk or do many other things. One scene remained in his memory that broke his heart. Poor Umm Nasir, she couldn't handle the stroke. The illness was too much for her to endure. This illness alone was her worry and fear. Delusions and nightmares filled up her mind.

(I didn't know if she had preferred death after the illness became worse and she became paralyzed. In any case it was up to God. She left me alone. Now poor Fawziyah is responsible for me. She is gentle like her mother.)

—God have mercy on her.

There was a continuous knock on the doctor's door although there was a small sign stating "Do not knock on the door."

The nurse came out. This time she swallowed her resentment and put on a fake smile, showing the teeth stained by glaring lipstick. She welcomed, with an unnatural gesture, two men who appeared to be important officials. She went back in with them and shut the door.

He looked at the clock. Time went by slowly. Pain continued to permeate his body, becoming impossible to tolerate.

He decided to go to the hospital manager. This situation is bad, very bad. He stood up and was ready to let the young man sit in his seat. So he decided to move over to him again. But the pain in his back and right knee reminded him again of their existence. Should he complain? But to whom? What's the use in complaining? It wouldn't work. Words, words disappear in the air. He remembered the doctor's warning about anger and distress. His blood pressure was about to rise.

He tried to distract himself with pleasant thoughts of the following day. Fawziyah would come to visit and would spend most of the day with him, as she did every week. She would bring her children, Badr, Fahd, and Fawaz.

He mentally mumbled to himself.

—I hope God will grant her a daughter and name her after Sara. Umm Nasir. Sara Khalid is deep in my memory. Sara, my sweetheart and wife. She was my first and would be the last. God have mercy on her. Poor Fawziyah is very tired from taking care of her husband, home, and children. Let alone my doctor's appointments, medicine, food, cleaning the house. Managing all these responsibilities is very overwhelming. But she never complains. May God protect her.

He was brought back from his state of reverie by the sound of heated arguing. An angry and muffled voice protesting the long wait.

—Service interruption. Service interruption. What's going on is annoying. When will this service interruption be over? This is wrong. We've been here since seven. We're awaiting our turn. We're undergoing pain. In the meantime, we see these people entering the doctor's room in spite of us. Where is the respect for the proper order? This is chaos, chaos.

The nurse, who was standing by another doctor's room entrance, looked at him and reacted to the situation with an unsettling coldness. In the middle of her chewing, which she did in an odd way, she spewed out some words:

—The hospital manager is in the first room. You may forward your complaint. I can't help you. It isn't your turn yet. You want order . . . She raised her hand, which showed a large portion was covered by golden bracelets. She pointed at the patients sitting there.

—They all are waiting like you and they are all patients. She turned to them ignoring his yelling and called the next patient's name.

—Mansur Abd Al-Rahman. Mansur Abd al-Rahman. After a while, the nurse came out from the doctor's office. Abu Nasir jumped up and was prepared to hear his name called.

—Basyuni Abd Al-Salam. Basyuni Abd Al-Salam.

The nurse gave a big smile as Basyuni approached. She asked him questions in a friendly manner.

—How are your wife and children? She finished the conversation, entered the room with him, and shut the door.

Abu Nasir couldn't hold it in any more and uttered a low yell only he could hear and then a deep sigh.

—There is no solution yet. Good Lord. I am just a Kuwaiti and nothing else.

The pain in both regions—the lower back and the right knee—was getting worse. He put his thin hands on the painful spots and pressed hard. Perhaps they did respond to his weakness, the pain actually faded.

He raised his voice and uttered a phrase in order to control the irritating situation that just might cause him a heart attack at any moment:

—There is no god but God. Muhammad is the Messenger of God.

* * *

Departure

I feel inadequate when I see some children of my age playing in the yard near our house. I sit around the corner of our house and watch them. I hear their laughter and see the ball bouncing among them.

—Come on, Umar! Come to play with us.

—Thanks. I don't like soccer.

I am lying. I love soccer and am addicted to the games on television. But how can I tell them that I can't play with them because of my poor health? My mother has warned me so. Poor mom is just doing what she is told by the doctor.

—Umar, don't play strenuous games. You'll get sick.

I will get sick . . . That phrase frightens me. I know I can get sick from the most trivial cause.

I like going to the beach. My mother does, too. She is very happy to know that we both love the sea. It is even better when we go together with my aunt. We spread a rug and sit on the beach. I position my scrawny body toward the sea and start talking to it about my concerns. I challenge its power and vastness.

I put my hand in the sea, trying to put some water in my mouth. It is very salty. I make a paper boat and send it off so that it can start its journey in the sea. I hope the waves won't swallow it because although it is weak like me, it carries my wishes and determination. I am letting my dreams and ambitions travel on the back of this little paper boat . . . Small and big things are leaving me for a journey to the unknown.

Sometimes, I am scared of the sea. Other times I am not. Two fighting feelings go back and forth. I throw myself on the cold sand, looking in the sky and the stars. I hear my mother saying from behind:

—Be careful of the cold sand, Umar.

Be careful. Be careful. Be careful, mother, not to be so careful with me. I have completed the journey that I began. I look at my boat, which still manages to withstand the small waves that are trying to overturn it. I love my small boat because it has strong will, which is a part of my own. I see a bird of dreams fly by me, big and strong. I have changed into one.

I feel the cold of the sand. I circle around, facing the sea with my back. My mother is still talking to my aunt, a long chat between women that never ends. Seconds have passed, in which I think about the plan that I would like to bring to school next week. My teacher Hasan believes in my academic creativity. He always encourages me. I have even received a certificate of the top prize. The students' applause won't leave my memory. I should not disappoint him.

I remember my paper boat, so I circle around. Where is my boat? Where is it? Ah! It still manages to withstand the challenges of the waves. I am so happy that I have forgotten the cold of the sand. How admirable you are, my boat!

*   *   *

Who Listens to My Voice?

My father always complained to me about his bad health when he was aging and had retired from work. My mother was tormented by sad thoughts in her memory, in which the male relatives from her family were political prisoners.

As for me, I was very skinny and my facial features showed melancholy and distress between my sad eyes.

My skin color was dark and my face wouldn't attract men's attention. When I saw the beautiful girls next door, I felt so different from them. They made fun of my clothes and of the face that showed my misery. I couldn't hide the pimples scattered on my face.

—Her mother works as a servant for other houses.

I didn't know, but I felt like a bug that irritated everyone.

My father decided to travel to a nearby country. I also wanted to escape from reality. My childhood had gone from me early. I never knew the taste of fun.

I said farewell to my painful memory. I wanted to forget the screams of the girls in my neighborhood and the harsh looks they gave me.

My father used to work as a shepherd in the desert. He took care of a large flock of sheep for a businessman for a very small wage. He spent with us a little time every week. As for my mother, she did housekeeping regularly in one of the businessmen's houses.

I was left alone. I indulged myself in school textbooks and dedicated myself completely to reading and writing. I would become a shining star. I would challenge everyone and wouldn't work as a housekeeper in businessmen's houses.

My mother came to me one day with a smile on her face.

—Zahrah, I have a surprise for you.

She carried a bag, staring at me smiling before opening the bag.

—Zahrah, close your eyes. I closed my eyes. Something quickly passed by—a little bug flying in front of me. I stayed away. How disgusting bugs were!

I opened my eyes.

—Umm Khalid, may God repay her. She gave me these nice clothes for you. They were her daughter Hissah's.

My mother showed me the clothes. Her image faded and voice vanished. I dived headlong into another world.

We lived in garbage. Lots of garbage.

Disgusting insects always flew in front of me. I couldn't get rid of them or kill them all off. I would kill some everyday. For that thought I had a smile that no one noticed.

Years passed by and I tolerated the bitterness of the searing looks that were tossed at me by my classmates. I didn't have any friend. I was always alone in the schoolyard. I always heard hurtful expressions:

—She is a foreigner to us. She is a spy. Be careful with her. Girls exchanged their murmurs with each other. I heard it like a scream burning my ears.

—Did you see the tattoo above . . .

—Yes.

A sneering laugh entered my ears, tearing me to pieces inside. I was destroyed and felt like crumbling away.

A voice joined to continue the conversation.

—She is from there . . .

—Why did she come? We don't want her around.

—I hope she leaves. I stayed in one of the corners in the open yard, wishing I could hide at that moment.

My father died one night of extreme cold. He said goodbye to the world and left us. Had we become part of this country? No. Those harassing looks made sure that we were not one of them.

I had forgotten my dialect and old identity. Or perhaps I was trying to forget everything.

Those annoying insects stayed with me, accompanying me and living inside me.

I looked at myself in the mirror. I saw the tattoo. I remembered the pain. When I was younger, I believed that it would add a touch of beauty that I didn't have. I should have taken it off.

I decided to keep that imprint of the past, which reminded me of the sorrow of my childhood. I decided that I could do without my old identity, but they rejected me still.

I came out from the hospital as a new person, although the tattoo remained.

A warm breeze caressed me. I smelled new perfume.

—I am no longer a stranger here. I will carry out my dreams.

At night I was embraced by dreams. A voice called me from afar that night.

—Zahrah. Wake up and write.

I woke up. I heard my mother Suad and saw college books scattered on the floor.

—I smell the odor of water fermenting the cracks in the wall . . .

I picked a pen and paper and wrote down my first poem. I finished it and slept so deeply for the first time in my life.

My teacher who escaped from my country here asked me to read my poem.

—A beautiful poem. Zahrah you are a poet. You'll become a shining star in the sky of poetry.

—But they reject me.

She responded harshly to me:

—Who rejects you?

I changed my mind.

—No one. I am just talking nonsense.

I left her office, feeling happy. I wetted my paper with tears.

*   *   *

Author's Biography

Haifa Al Sanousi is an author and a faculty member of the College of Arts at Kuwait University. She received a Ph.D. in modern Arabic literature and literary criticism from the University of Glasgow in the U.K. She also has studied in Egypt and Tunisia, and traveled extensively to present papers at academic symposia and conferences.

Al Sanousi has published an extensive number of books. These include:

- *Al-Qissah al-Kuwaytiyah Shaklan wa Madmunan (Kuwaiti Stories: Form and Content)*
- *Shi'r Khalifah al-Waqiyan bayna al-Mawqif wa al-Fikri wa al-Bina' al-Fanni (Khalid al-Waqiyan's Poems: Between Position, Thought, and Art Form)*
- *Muqtatafat min al-Shi'r al-Kuwayti (Selections of Kuwaiti Poetry)*
- *The Echo of Kuwaiti Creativity*
- *Women in a Swirl: A Collection of Stories*
- *Al-Anisah Razan wa Tabib al-Asnan: Majmu'ah qisasiyah lil-Atfal (Lady Razan and Dr. al-Asnan: A Collection of Children's Stories)*
- *A Knock on Our Door (Qissah lil-Atfal bil-Ishtirak ma'a Ilena Ramisi: Children's Stories Co-authored with Ilena Ramisi)*
- *Kalimatuk Qad Tughayyir Hayatik, bil-Ishtirak ma'a Dr. James Binibkr (Your Words Could Change Your Life)*
- *Dajij (Noise)*
- *The Moment of Silence*
- *Al-Kitabah al-Ta'biriyah: Kurrasah Tamrinat 'Amaliyah (Expressive Writing: A Workbook)*

In addition to the above, Al Sanousi has presented many research papers in both Arabic and English at seminars and conferences at universities both inside and outside the Arab world on therapeutic writing. Her website on creative expression and healing is: http://www.razan.com/.

Translator's Biography

Dr. Anchi Hoh holds a Ph.D and an MA in Middle Eastern Studies (University of Manchester), an MA in Jewish Studies (Gratz College), a Certificate in Arab Studies (Kuwait University), an MLS from the University of Maryland, College Park, and a BA in Arabic Language and Literature from the National Chengchi University, Taipei, Taiwan. Dr. Hoh has published extensively on Middle East Studies. Her doctoral dissertation deals with the image of Arab women in contemporary Kuwaiti women's short stories from the 70s to the present. Dr. Hoh is Editor of *Journal of Middle East and Islamic Studies in Asia* (JMEISA).

www.ingramcontent.com/pod-product-compliance
Lightning Source LLC
Chambersburg PA
CBHW021257280526
45784CB00005B/2407